The Mississippi River

The Largest River in the United States

Janeen R. Adil

WEIGL PUBLISHERS INC.

Published by Weigl Publishers Inc.
350 5th Avenue, Suite 3304
New York, NY 10118-0069
USA

Web site: www.weigl.com

Library of Congress Cataloging-in-Publication Data

Adil, Janeen R.
  The Mississippi River / Janeen R. Adil.
    v. cm. -- (Natural wonders of the USA)
Includes bibliographical references (p.) and index.
Contents: A river of wonders -- Where in the world? -- A trip back in time -- Water at work -- Life along the river -- Early explorers -- The big picture -- People of the river -- The river's heritage -- Must see and do -- Key issues: changes on the Mississippi River -- Timelines -- What have you learned?
  ISBN 1-59036-041-9 (Library Bound : alk. paper) – ISBN 1-59036-163-6 (pbk.)
  1. Mississippi River--Juvenile literature. [1. Mississippi River.] I. Title. II. Series.
  F351 .A34 2003
  977--dc21
                                    2002013644
Printed in the United States of America
1 2 3 4 5 6 7 8 9 0 07 06 05 04 03

Project Coordinators
Michael Lowry
Tina Schwartzenberger

Copy Editor
Frances Purslow

Design
Terry Paulhus

Layout
Virginia Boulay

Photo Researchers
Nicole Bezic King
Wendy Cosh

Photograph Credits

Every reasonable effort has been made to trace ownership and to obtain permission to reprint copyright material. The publishers would be pleased to have any errors or omissions brought to their attention so that they may be corrected in subsequent printings.

Cover: The Mississippi River (**Clint Farlinger**); **Corel Corporation:** pages 9T, 9M, 10T, 10TM, 10BM, 10B, 12, 25L, 25R, 26B; **Clint Farlinger:** pages 1, 4, 8, 13, 24, 26T; **Georgia Historical Society:** page 14; **Hannibal Convention and Visitors Bureau:** page 27R; **Bruce Leighty:** page 23; **Louisiana Department of Tourism:** page 28; **Map Resources:** page 5; **Memphis Convention and Visitors Bureau:** page 21; **Steve Mulligan:** page 6; **National Archives of Canada:** page 15 (C-5066); **Photofest:** page 20; **USGS/EROS Data Center:** page 9B; **Marilyn "Angel" Wynn:** page 18, 19, 27L.

Contents

The Mighty Mississippi

The Mississippi River is the largest river in North America. It supplies water to millions of people. People and wildlife need the river for drinking water, and farmers use it to water their crops. No wonder this river is often called the Mighty Mississippi!

On a map, the Mississippi River appears to divide the United States. The river has actually brought the country together. Before there were cars and trains, the Mississippi River was a major transportation route. Settlers used canoes to travel to new parts of the land. Native Peoples, and later the Europeans, settled along its banks.

The Mississippi River begins its journey in Minnesota and empties into the Gulf of Mexico from Louisiana.

Mississippi River Facts:

• The Mississippi River is 2,340 miles long. That is as long as 322,000 school buses parked end to end!

• The Mississippi River borders ten states.

• Streams and rivers from thirty-one states drain into the Mississippi River.

• The Mississippi River's **basin** makes up 40 percent of the land in the U.S.

• About 12 million people live along the Mississippi River.

• Every second, 612,000 cubic feet of water is discharged from the Mississippi River into the Gulf of Mexico.

The Mississippi River Locator

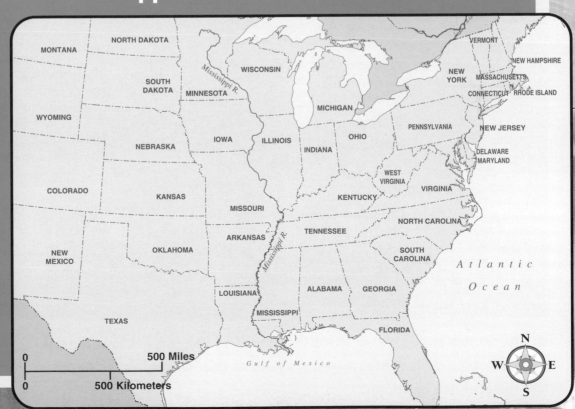

Where in the World?

The Mississippi River is divided into three parts. It begins as a stream small enough to step over. The stream flows out of Lake Itasca in northern Minnesota. This section is called the Headwaters. It ends at St. Anthony Falls, near the twin cities of St. Paul and Minneapolis.

The next section, known as the Upper Mississippi, flows from St. Anthony Falls to Cairo, Illinois. The Upper Mississippi River flows through Wisconsin, Iowa, and Missouri. In St. Louis, Missouri, the great Missouri River joins the Mississippi River.

The Gateway Arch straddles the banks of the Mississippi River in St. Louis. The arch commemorates the city's role as the "Gateway to the West" during the nineteenth century.

Puzzler

The Mississippi River is one of the most important bodies of water in the United States.

Q What are some of the other major rivers and lakes of the United States?

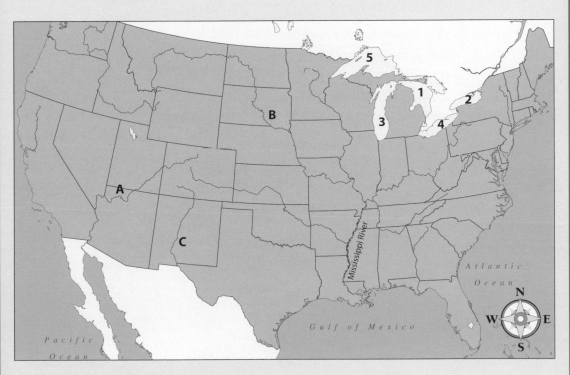

Great Lakes:
1. Lake Huron
2. Lake Ontario
3. Lake Michigan
4. Lake Erie
5. Lake Superior

 Rivers:
A. The Colorado River
B. The Missouri River
C. The Rio Grande

A Trip Back in Time

Nearly 2 million years ago, **glaciers** covered parts of North America. Their movement was a major force in shaping the Mississippi River. These gigantic ice sheets were at least 1 mile thick. The Wisconsin glacier was the last of the great glaciers in the area.

About 10,000 to 12,000 years ago, the Wisconsin glacier shrank toward the north. Its movement carved out parts of the Mississippi riverbed. The melting glacier also left large amounts of water, which formed the Mississippi River, as well as streams and lakes. The glacier also wore away rocks and left sediment behind. The changing landscape continued to alter the Mississippi River's shape.

Water and mud flow from the Missouri River into the Mississippi River, giving the Mississippi the nickname "The Big Muddy."

Anatomy of a River

What has branches, a trunk, and roots? A tree—and a river! A river also has parts called branches, trunk, and roots. A river's branches, trunk, and roots are different from those of a tree.

Branches
Branches flowing into a river are called **tributaries**. As these streams flow into a river, they bring water and **sediment**. The Missouri River is a major tributary to the Mississippi River.

Trunk
A river's trunk is its main channel. Water and sediment move along the river's channel to the ocean.

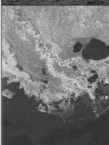

Roots
A river's roots are the streams that empty into its **delta**. Here, sediment and water flow into the ocean. Sediment is also left behind in the delta. The Mississippi Delta is an area of rich, flat land where cotton, rice, and soybeans are grown.

Water at Work

Water is the most precious resource on Earth. All living things depend on it. Earth is covered by more water than land. About 97 percent of Earth's water is salt water in the oceans. The remaining 3 percent is fresh water. However, two-thirds of the fresh water is frozen in glaciers and ice caps. Only about one-third of the fresh water is available for use by people and land animals.

Earth recycles its water. This means that humans are using the same water that dinosaurs did! The **water cycle** describes the way water moves above, on, and below the ground. The cycle has four stages.

Storage
Water can be stored in the ground and in oceans, lakes, and rivers. It can also be stored in glaciers and ice caps.

Evaporation
When water evaporates, it changes from a liquid to a gas, or vapor. Heat makes water evaporate more quickly.

Precipitation
Water vapor collects in clouds. It then falls to the ground as precipitation, such as rain or snow. Every day, precipitation is falling somewhere in the world.

Runoff
Runoff is precipitation that flows into rivers and streams. The water reaches them by flowing either on or through the ground. Heavy rains result in runoff. Floods may occur when a river cannot hold all this water.

The Water Cycle

The Mississippi River is part of the water cycle. The stages of the water cycle are described on the previous page. Because it is a river, water is stored in the Mississippi. Water also evaporates from the river, forming clouds. When the clouds cannot hold more moisture, precipitation falls from them, entering the Mississippi River once again. Finally, when the Mississippi River becomes too full, water runoff may cause flooding.

The illustration below shows how the Mississippi River is involved in the water cycle.

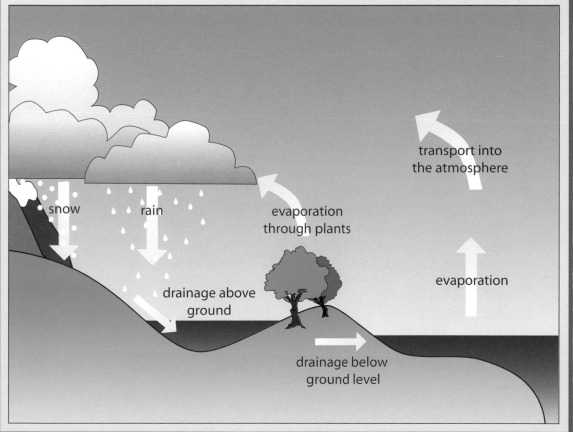

snow

rain

evaporation through plants

transport into the atmosphere

evaporation

drainage above ground

drainage below ground level

Life Along the River

More than 400 species of wildlife live along or in the Mississippi River. Each section of the river has its own species and habitats.

In the north, pine and spruce forests line the Headwaters. This is where bear, elk, moose, and wolves make their homes. Overhead, eagles and snowy owls soar over beds of wild rice.

The Upper Mississippi includes many different habitats. Among them are lakes, marshes, forests, and beaches. Part of this area is protected as a national **refuge**.

Along the Lower Mississippi, the land is flat. The warmer climate and plentiful rainfall make this a more tropical area.

Habitat destruction and over-hunting are serious threats to the black bear, once common along the Lower Mississippi.

River Ecosystems

A special type of **ecosystem** occurs where the Lower Mississippi drains into the Gulf of Mexico. This is an area of coastal **wetlands**, where fresh water and salt water meet.

These wetlands are home to fish, crabs, shrimp, oysters, shore birds, and many other animals. Cypress trees drip with Spanish moss. Mangrove trees sink their roots into the water. Many alligators live in the saltwater marshes.

Early Explorers

The first European to see the Mississippi River was Hernando de Soto, in 1541. He left Spain in search of gold. De Soto and his 600-person crew explored southeastern Florida without finding gold. Soon after crossing the Mississippi River, de Soto died and was buried in the river.

Other early explorers came from France. In 1673, Father Jacques Marquette and Louis Joliet canoed down the Mississippi River. They were the first Europeans to follow the river south to the Arkansas River. Joliet, an excellent mapmaker, mapped out their travels along the Mississippi River.

Memphis, Tennessee, is thought to be the location where Hernando de Soto and his crew first saw the Mississippi River.

Biography

René Robert Cavelier, Sieur de La Salle (1643–1687)

René Robert Cavelier, Sieur de La Salle, was another French explorer who traveled the Mississippi River. French King Louis XIV gave him permission to explore the river down to its mouth. Along the way, La Salle could establish forts and trading posts.

La Salle traveled the river by canoe, reaching the Gulf of Mexico in 1682. He claimed the land for France. In honor of his king, La Salle named the area Louisiana.

In 1803, the United States bought the Louisiana Territory from France. The sale included more than 820,000 square miles of land, along with the Mississippi River. Called the Louisiana Purchase, this sale made the United States one of the largest nations in the world. In 1812, Louisiana became a state.

Facts of Life

Born: November 1643

Hometown: Rouen, France

Occupation: trader, soldier, explorer

Died: January 1687

The Big Picture

Large rivers are found all over the world. This map shows each continent's major river. Even the frozen continent of Antarctica has rivers of ice.

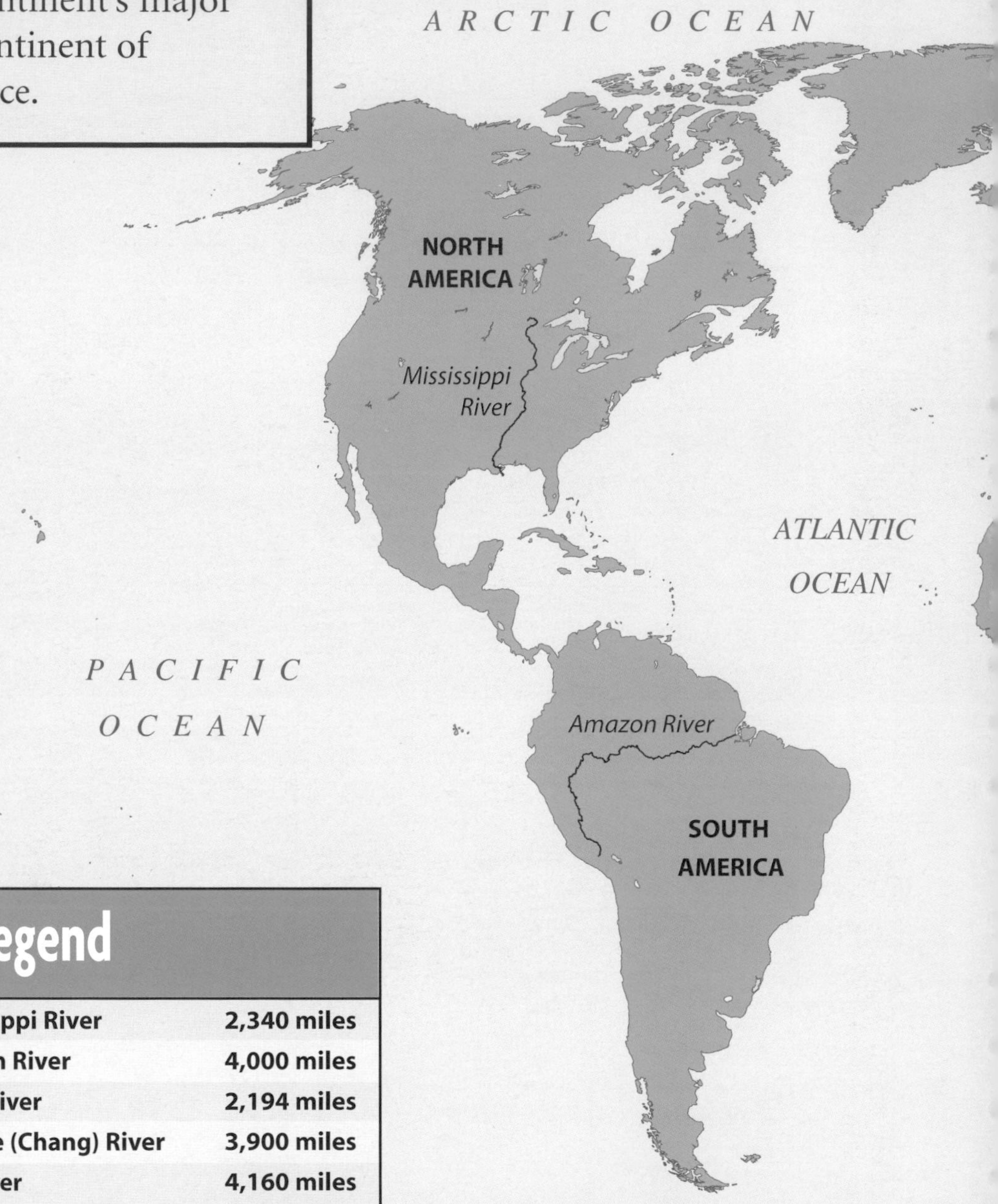

ARCTIC OCEAN

NORTH
AMERICA

Mississippi
River

ATLANTIC
OCEAN

PACIFIC
OCEAN

Amazon River

SOUTH
AMERICA

Map Legend

North America	Mississippi River	2,340 miles
South America	Amazon River	4,000 miles
Europe	Volga River	2,194 miles
Asia	Yangtze (Chang) River	3,900 miles
Africa	Nile River	4,160 miles
Australia	Murray River	1,566 miles
Antarctica (not shown)	Onyx River	12 miles

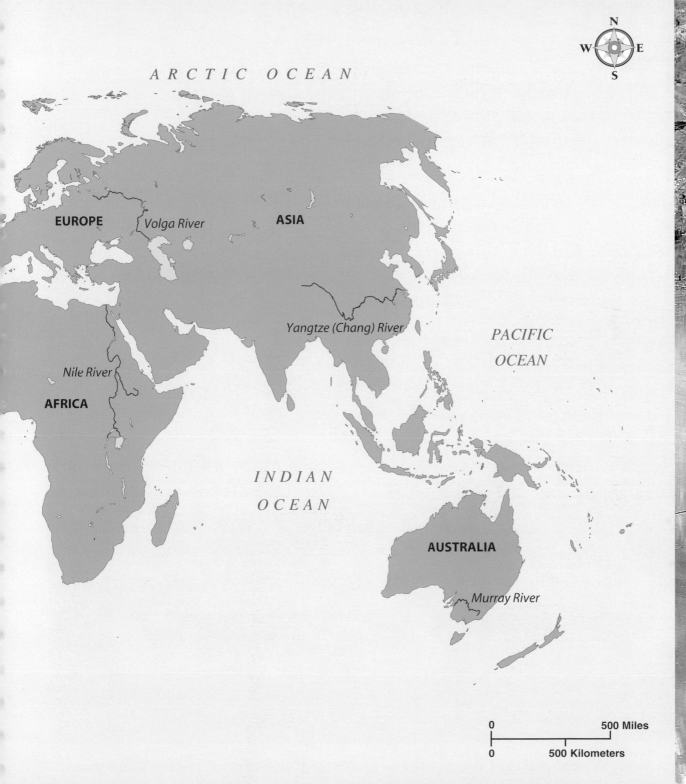

ARCTIC OCEAN

EUROPE

Volga River

ASIA

Yangtze (Chang) River

PACIFIC
OCEAN

Nile River

AFRICA

INDIAN
OCEAN

AUSTRALIA

Murray River

N
W E
S

0   500 Miles

0   500 Kilometers

People of the River

People have lived along the Mississippi River for thousands of years. Native Americans built communities throughout the area. They fished its waters and hunted birds and animals along its shores. When the river overflowed, rich sediment was left on the **floodplain**, which created soil ideal for farming.

The Ojibwa of northern Minnesota named the river *misi sipi*, which means "great river." The Cherokee, Chickasaw, Choctaw, Creek, and Seminole made their homes in the South. In the early part of the nineteenth century, the United States Army forced many of these groups to leave their homes. Their journey west of the Mississippi River is known as the "Trail of Tears."

Many descendants of the Southern Mississippi tribes now live in Oklahoma, a result of their forced journey, the "Trail of Tears."

Birchbark Canoes

Native Americans used canoes to travel along the Mississippi River. Canoes were fast and quiet on the water. Many Native groups in the northeast built a special kind of light, graceful canoe. The canoe's frame was usually white cedar wood. The frame was covered with sheets of bark cut from birch trees. The birchbark sheets were sewn together with spruce tree roots. Then, thick tree sap was rubbed over the canoe to make it waterproof.

Other nations, such as those of the southeast, made dugout canoes. These canoes were created by hollowing out a large tree trunk or log.

When European explorers arrived, they saw how useful these Native-American boats were. The Europeans decided to use canoes for traveling the Mississippi River.

River Stories

The Mississippi River has inspired many writers. Mark Twain's stories are the best known. Twain grew up in Hannibal, Missouri, a town along the Mississippi River. Mark Twain loved the river and wrote about it in many of his books. He thought the Mississippi River had "a new story to tell every day."

In 1876, Twain published *The Adventures of Tom Sawyer*. In 1884, Twain wrote *The Adventures of Huckleberry Finn*, which has come to be his most popular book. Some of the most exciting events in *The Adventures of Huckleberry Finn* take place on the Mississippi River. Huck and his friend Jim escape capture by sailing down the river on a raft. Both of these books are still popular today.

■ Mark Twain, whose real name was Samuel Langhorne Clemens, once worked as a steamboat pilot on the Mississippi River. His experiences provided material for many of his books.

Music of the Mississippi

African Americans living in the Mississippi Delta developed a type of music called the blues. They based this music on work songs and spirituals created by African Americans who had been made to work as slaves. The blues are usually slow, moody songs with a strong rhythm. The songs communicate African-American experiences.

Another type of music, known as jazz, developed out of the blues. Jazz became popular in the early 1900s in the city of New Orleans, Louisiana. People still travel to New Orleans to hear the many excellent jazz bands.

Natural Attractions

There are many things to see and do on a visit to the Mississippi River. There are wonderful restaurants, festivals, and sporting opportunities, such as fishing.

Try some Creole and Cajun foods in New Orleans. Creole cooking is a delicious mix of African, French, German, Haitian, Italian, Native-American, and Spanish flavors. Cajun cooking often combines meat, seafood, and vegetables. Creole and Cajun food was first developed in Louisiana.

Another popular activity is fishing for catfish. The Mississippi River is full of catfish, named for their long "whiskers."

If you are in Hannibal, Missouri, in July, be sure to attend the National Tom Sawyer Days. This festival has delighted visitors since 1956. A fence-painting contest is just one of the many fun festival activities.

Crispy Fried Catfish (serves 6)

Ask a teacher or parent to help you make this delicious Southern dish.

- 6 skinned catfish
- 1/2 cup evaporated milk
- 1 tablespoon salt
- dash pepper

- 1 cup flour
- 1/2 cup yellow cornmeal
- 2 teaspoons paprika
- 12 slices bacon

Clean, wash, and dry the fish. Combine milk, salt, and pepper in one bowl. Combine flour, cornmeal, and paprika in another bowl. Dip fish in the milk mixture and roll in the flour mixture. Fry bacon in a heavy pan until it is crisp. Remove bacon and drain it on a paper towel. Reserve the fat for frying fish. Fry fish in the hot fat for 4 minutes. Turn the fish over and fry for 4 to 6 minutes longer, or until the fish is brown and flakes easily. Pat the fish with a paper towel. Serve fish with bacon.

Source: *The Mississippi Cookbook*

Paddle Steamers

"Steamboat's a-comin'!" At one time, this excited cry could be heard up and down the Mississippi River. Steamboats, or paddle steamers, ruled the river. These long, tall boats carried people and cargo. Wood fires heated the huge boilers. The boilers, in turn, produced steam, moving the great paddle wheels.

The first steamboat to travel down the Mississippi River, the *New Orleans*, sailed in 1811. By the 1850s, more than 3,000 paddle steamers were docking at the port of New Orleans. The *Delta Queen* continues to offer visitors a chance to cruise the Mississippi River on a traditional paddle steamer. This beautiful steamboat is a National Historic Landmark.

Controlling the Flow

Floods and droughts are important to wildlife habitats along the Mississippi River. However, humans have changed the Mississippi River. Dams, **locks**, and **levees** have been built along the river to control the flow of river water. The Mississippi, with its important role in the water cycle, must be protected. By keeping the river healthy, people and wildlife can share and enjoy this wonderful river.

▬ Lock and Dam No. 9 is one of twenty-nine locks and dams located on the Upper Mississippi.

Many people believe that the Mississippi River needs to be managed with care. There is a need to work together to clean up the water, restore floodplains, and protect habitats and ecosystems. Communities have a role in caring for their sections of the river. State and federal governments must work together on dam and flood control projects.

Should humans control the course of the Mississippi River?

YES	NO
Dams and levees created large areas of agricultural land along the river.	Millions of acres of wetlands have been drained. This damages the environment and threatens wildlife.
Dams and levees help keep the river from flooding farms, towns, and cities.	Changes in the river's flow mean sediment either settles in the wrong places or is washed away.
Locks make it possible for boats to easily carry cargo up and down the river. 	Floods are a natural part of life along the Mississippi River, and dams and levees cannot prevent all of them. 

Time Line

5–4 billion years ago
Earth is formed.

600–300 million years ago
Seas rise and fall over the
North American continent.

300–200 million years ago
Dinosaurs and mammals
begin to evolve.

250 million years ago
The course of the Lower
Mississippi is established.

65 million years ago
Dinosaurs become extinct.

1.8–1.5 million years ago
Glaciers move forward,
then back.

The Mississippi valley has rich soils formed by thousands of years
of erosion and river deposits. The soils support plant life very well.

The Mississippi River has flooded several times in recent history.

1.5 million years ago
The Upper Mississippi forms.

120,000 years ago
The first modern
humans evolve.

100,000–75,000 years ago
The Wisconsin
glacier advances.

12,700 years ago
The great Upper Mississippi
flood begins.

12,000–10,000 years ago
The Wisconsin
glacier retreats.

1541
Hernando de Soto is the
first European to see the
Mississippi River.

1673
Father Jacques Marquette
and Louis Joliet canoe
down the Mississippi as
far as Arkansas.

Numerous Native Peoples have lived along the banks of the Mississippi River. These are the people who gave the Mississippi River its name.

In the area around Hannibal, Missouri, it is common to see people celebrating Mark Twain's book *Tom Sawyer*. This boy is dressed as Tom Sawyer in honor of the book.

1830s–1870s
This period is the "golden age" of steamboats.

1861–1865
During the Civil War, the Mississippi River is used by Northern armies to invade the South. It is the scene of many important battles.

1914
A dam built at Keokuk, Iowa, produces hydroelectric power.

1927
The largest flood in the recorded history of the Mississippi River occurs in the lower valley.

1930s
Dams with locks are built to deepen the main channel to 9 feet.

1993
A flood on the Upper Mississippi River causes billions of dollars in damage.

2001
Another large and serious flood happens on the Upper Mississippi.

1682
René Robert Cavelier, Sieur de La Salle, reaches the Gulf of Mexico.

1803
The United States receives the Mississippi River from France as part of the Louisiana Purchase.

1811
The *New Orleans* is the first steamboat to travel the Mississippi River.

1835
Mark Twain is born in Florida, Missouri.

What Have You Learned?

True or False?

Decide whether the following statements are true or false. If the statement is false, make it true.

1. About 100 species of wildlife live in or on the river.

2. Creole and Cajun cooking developed in Minnesota.

3. The Mississippi River begins as a tiny stream.

4. Hernando de Soto gave Louisiana its name.

5. Travelers can still ride on the *Delta Queen*.

6. Cotton is grown in the Mississippi Delta.

7. Land covers most of Earth.

ANSWERS

1. False. About 400 species of wildlife live on or in the Mississippi River.

2. False. Creole and Cajun cooking developed in Louisiana.

3. True.

4. False. René Cavalier, Sieur de La Salle, named Louisiana.

5. True.

6. True.

7. False. Water covers most of Earth.

Short Answer

Answer the following questions using information from the book.

1. What are the three sections of the Mississippi River?

2. In the water cycle, where does fresh water come from?

3. Who wrote *The Adventures of Tom Sawyer*?

4. In what year did La Salle reach the mouth of the Mississippi River?

5. What are the names of the Great Lakes?

6. What are three human structures that help control the Mississippi River?

ANSWERS

1. The Headwaters, the Upper Mississippi, and the Lower Mississippi
2. Fresh water falls as rain or snow
3. Mark Twain
4. 1682
5. Lake Huron, Lake Ontario, Lake Michigan, Lake Erie, and Lake Superior
6. Dams, locks, and levees

Multiple Choice

Choose the best answer in the following multiple choice questions.

1. Jazz developed out of what type of music?

   a) rap
   b) rock
   c) blues
   d) classical

2. Native Americans built what kind of boat for traveling the river?

   a) steamboat
   b) canoe
   c) rowboat
   d) ship

3. "Mississippi" comes from Ojibwa, meaning what?

   a) "long water"
   b) "wide river"
   c) "river of mud"
   d) "great river"

4. In prehistoric times, what helped carve out the Mississippi River?

   a) glaciers
   b) tidal waves
   c) storms
   d) floods

1.c, 2.b, 3.d, 4.a

ANSWERS

Find Out for Yourself

Books

Lourie, Peter. *Mississippi River*. Pennsylvania: Boyds Mills Press, 2000.

Mudd Ruth, Maria. *The Mississippi River*. New York: Benchmark Books, 2001.

Twain, Mark. *The Adventures of Huckleberry Finn*. New Jersey: Princeton Review, 2001.

Web Sites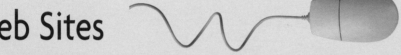

Use the Internet to find out more about the people, plants, and animals of the Mississippi River.

U.S. Environmental Protection Agency
www.epa.gov/region07/kids/wtrcycle.htm
This Web site describes how the water cycle works.

American Rivers
www.amrivers.org
This organization works to protect and restore rivers in the United States.

Encarta
http://encarta.msn.com
Search this online encyclopedia to find out more about the Mississippi River.

Skill Matching Page

What did you learn? Look at the questions in the "Skills" column. Compare them to the page number of the answers in the "Page" column. Refresh your memory by reading the "Answer" column below.

SKILLS	ANSWER	PAGE
What facts did I learn from this book?	I learned that about 12 million people live along the Mississippi River.	5
What skills did I learn?	I learned how to read maps.	5, 7, 16–17
What activities did I do?	I answered the questions in the quiz.	28–29
How can I find out more?	I can read the books and visit the Web sites on the Find Out for Yourself page.	30
How can I get involved?	I can fish the Mississippi River or make a southern dish.	22

Glossary

basin: the region draining into a river
delta: a large, triangle-shaped area at the mouth of a river
ecosystem: a community of plants, animals, and their environment
floodplain: low, flat land that is flooded by a river
glaciers: large masses of moving ice
levees: riverbanks built by people to prevent flooding
locks: gates closing off part of a river; the water level is raised or lowered so boats can pass through
refuge: a protected area
sediment: mud, sand, and pieces of rock that are moved by water
tributaries: streams that flow into a river
water cycle: circular movement of water through ground and sky
wetlands: low, wet wildlife habitat area, such as a marsh or swamp

Index